Wind ... Be Faithful to Me

by

Anthony Brown

Copyright © 2006 by Anthony (Shepherd) Brown

Wind ... Be Faithful to Me
by Anthony (Shepherd) Brown

Printed in the United States of America

ISBN 1-60034-572-7

All rights reserved solely by the author. The author guarantees all contents are original and do not infringe upon the legal rights of any other person or work. No part of this book may be reproduced in any form without the permission of the author. The views expressed in this book are not necessarily those of the publisher.

Scripture taken from the HOLY BIBLE, NEW INTERNATIONAL VERSION®. Copyright © 1973, 1978, 1984 International Bible Society. Used by permission of Zondervan. All rights reserved.

www.xulonpress.com

The wind blows to the south turns to the north round and round it goes ever returning it' course.
Ecclesiastes 1:16

The wind blows wherever it pleases. You hear its sound, but you cannot tell where it comes from or where it is going. So it is with everyone born of the Spirit.
John 3:8

Who gave the ocean's waves it's boundaries…tells the waters to go no further?
— *Shepherd*

Introduction

I was talking with a man today at work. It could have been any person; it could have been any day. "I don't get it," he said. "If he didn't do anything, why did he have to suffer like that and die? He was a good man. He didn't harm anyone. Why did God let him die like that?"

Does this remind you of other conversations? Have you heard questions like this about Jesus before? If you feel as if this man has similar resentments toward religion, God, and/or salvation, I wrote this book for you.

I told the man that Jesus' life was the price for the redemption of humankind. "But that isn't right!" he said. "Do you think that is right? That isn't fair! Why did they kill him?"

"We killed him," I said. "Our sins caused him to die. Our darkness couldn't comprehend the light of his life. We rejected him—society, humankind."

You'd really have to be in hibernation for a long time to not be familiar with the information spoken in this conversation, yet it is still puzzling. It still sends shivers up your arms. It still causes our hair to stand straight up. Why? Why, God ... why? With such a controversial topic being discussed so adequately within our environment, you would think that we would get it by now, that we would understand the moral and the plot, and the whole story would be getting old. However, this very subject has confounded our world and deep theological thinkers for centuries. Why did Jesus die? And if that answer is found, what does it mean to us? Forgive me for beating a dead horse to the ground, but I will try to give you a better perspective to illumine the light of the reality of this story. No, for heaven's sake, I do not want to preach. But if you have a sincere heart and are honestly trying to understand the truth, I can help bring some light to this hard subject.

One thing I found when writing this book is that biblical quotes or scriptures used in the chapters were better understood as reflective thoughts or background voice (conscience) around the text in that particular part of the book. Even though some sections are written with one-half to two-thirds scripture reference, the words in the scriptures actually interpret the flow of thinking from the text and give you some biblical insight toward the genre.

Ironically, a Daily Devotion Handbook usually consists of a series of reflections, thoughts, or scripture quotes with text to give a better insight and/or understanding of God's word. This book is the reverse. The biblical quotes are not the main thoughts. I have a main focus or mindset to share on religion that I am trying to express to you without the scripture.

I wrote this book, proofread it, and found it difficult to follow. Nevertheless, I did see that I accomplished what I desired when I attempted to start writing this book. I question the flow when writing theological philosophy, especially when keeping it within a Christian perspective. Although some famous authors (such as C.S. Lewis) have captured the essence of deep Christian theology in simple everyday conversation, I still find it hard to mix. Although I question the art of writing non-fiction Christian theology so it is easy to understand, I am aware of the fact that one just may not consider my style of writing very good. Whether you have a hard time grasping "faith" or just reading my writing, I strongly suggest that you read this book at least twice. The first time you read it, you will get an overview of the total concept. Then place it down for a few days to a week and read it again for comprehension. Rather trusting in my writing or your own IQ, I promise if you attempt to look at spirituality from a different perspective and knowledge, you will be content. Whether you like this book or not, you will become aware of a keen eyesight on spiritual principles. You will find that I gave good thought to my words and prayed very deeply for interpretation and God's intercession on my words. You will not be disappointed with my work.

Table of Contents

Part 1: The Word 13

Chapter 1: The Logic of the Wind 15
    Section 1: The Word..15
    Section 2: His Reflection in the Mirror..................19
    Section 3: Opinion, Faith, and Beliefs...................23
    Section 4: Salvation: A Concept or Reality............27

Chapter 2: Why Cry to the Father? 31
    Section 1: Who Am I?...31
    Section 2: Knowing How to Drop to Your
        Knees..35
    Section 3: God's Mercy and Grace 39
    Section 4: Into His Hands 41

Chapter 3: Evangelism, Witnessing, and
        Testimonies...45

Part 2: The Relationship..51

Chapter 4: His Spirit in the Wind..................................53
    Section 1: Religions in the World 53

Section 2: The Bible: Face Value 57
Section 3: Christianity 61

Chapter 5: The Plan 65
Section 1: The Cross 65
Section 2: Our Nature, Our Sins 69
Section 3: In Conclusion 73

Part 3: Practical 75

Chapter 6: Seven Steps of Wisdom 77
Section 1: Praying 79
Section 2: Reading Scriptures 81
Section 3: Fellowship 85
Section 4: Fasting 89
Section 5: Writing 91
Section 6: Singing 93
Section 7: Tithing 95

Part 1

The Word

Chapter 1

The Logic of the Wind

Section 1: The Word

I arose in the morning with relief and excitement. After singing in the shower, I dressed myself, grabbed a quick brunch, and then headed outside to school. College was a real plus in my life at that time, and I did not want to lose the prestige. It impressed my family, ego, and associates, and I did not want to let go of the high. After going through a four-hour class on international cuisine, I indulged in the class project and then headed outside once again toward home. My home was not far away in those days—all I had to do was cut through the park and the Fort Wayne Coliseum's parking lot. I was resolved in the morning, but I was really looking forward to my four o'clock snack. Opening the door to my apartment (really my cousin's apartment; I could not afford rent anywhere else), I stepped into my utopia of a dream moment. Nothing in the morning, during the afternoon class, through the autumn breeze walk, or any other time in the history of my life was more pleasing to me than the next fifteen minutes. In the ashtray left on the floor after a hectic night was a small roach, also known as a small marijuana joint. I smoked it. It was now 4:00 P.M., and all the excitement was over. Everything I looked forward to in life was now gratified in fifteen minutes.

Now it became clear. Now I came to my senses—after fifteen years of active addiction, now I was content. That day of October 4, 1989, was the last time I lost my soul to addiction.

I did not see this day coming in my life. Ever since I was a child, I had some knowledge of God. I remember praying at my bedroom window at five o'clock in the morning while I watched the "azure" horizon. I recall talking to Him one afternoon in August 1989 outside my cousin's apartment on the steps. I just finished smoking a few marijuana cigarettes and was high. I left my hometown to start a fresh new life, but as if wearing a day-old diaper, I was swallowed in my own filth. It was then that I spoke to Him in a tree and said, "God, I don't know if this is a sin, but if it is not Your will, please give me a sign." The wind blew through the tree, and I said, "I don't know how or when, but I will give up smoking marijuana."

I was tired of the hassle, grief, and social antipathy. I had resentment toward life. I had resentment toward myself. I had resentment toward God. I hated how I was living and could not figure a way out. The door to deliverance was close while I stood still knocking. If I knew why Jesus was the key, I did not understand how to apply Him. This is where most people miss the mark. If God is real and powerful with thunder in His voice and lightning in His fist, why does it seem so hard to simply grasp His existence? You can understand the clouds and how they condense the air, but why bother to comprehend the wind? How is the very breath of life the answer to all creation in the present and throughout all time? I am amazed to know.

He spoke into absolute darkness and created light.

His words formed the foundation of the Earth.

He has blessed man as far as the stars are in heaven and in ways as countless as the grains of sand upon the ocean shore.

If there is any reason to a concept, then there is a cause. If life carries any meaning, then the creation has a purpose. The very being where this purpose is conceived holds the idea of hope, comfort, and all reality. This very fact makes the being formed in the creation complete. Everything is relative. Within the point of understanding life there is an answer that gives everything meaning. We just have to accept our place in the plan. God has everything in control.

"In the beginning was the Word, and the Word was with God, and the Word was God. He was with God in the beginning. Through him all things were made; without him nothing was made that has been made. In him was life, and that life was the light of men. The light shines in the darkness, but the darkness has not understood it" (John 1:1–5).

Section 2: His Reflection in the Mirror

Let us make man in our own image.

"Then God said, 'Let us make man in our image, in our likeness, and let them rule over the fish of the sea and the birds of the air, over the livestock, over all the earth, and over all the creatures that move along the ground'" (Genesis 1:26).

In our image let us create man.

As a mirror reflection of ourselves, let us create man.

Males and females, let us make human beings.

"So God created man in his own image, in the image of God he created him; male and female he created them" (Genesis 1:27).

Can you see this picture of God (as the Mormons have done) with two arms, two legs, two eyes, a nose, a mouth, and a smile; with laughter, a voice, and the ability to cry; and with emotions, a personality, and a way of thinking? God is a who, and in our image we reflect Him and His character. It is not so much to get caught up with the physical abstract of man and compare it to God's creation, but to see the whole nature of man as a creation. Man is created with a mind, a heart, and a spirit or soul. It is in these three parts that we are able to reflect God.

Just as advertising, public relations, and marketing collaborate together in business yet have distinctive aspects, the mind, heart, body, and soul have a corresponding relationship as well as independent characteristics. Understanding God in these dispositions helps us to understand the Holy Trinity: the Father, the Son, and the Holy Spirit.

It can be said that writing, reading, and speaking all collaborate together as communication. The heart, mind, body, and soul are similar. Thus, the heart is as writing, the mind is as reading, and the body is as speaking. The body uses all five senses (seeing, hearing, smelling, tasting, and feeling) to connect with the world. The soul can be considered the language that is being used. Therefore, those who know more than one language have a more complex communication network. The type of language used also helps to form the reality.

These examples are given so you may have a better perspective of God and His creation. Actually, the mind of God is the Father; He is the Creator of everything, and without Him nothing would have been created. God's heart can best be seen and exclusively understood through the birth, life, death, prophecy, and revelation of His Son, the Word, Jesus Christ. The body of God (or the body of Christ) is the church. The body (God's communication to the outside world) is actually His plan for man's salvation. As you observe His Son and see God's Word throughout man's history in the Bible, you can better relate to His heart and mindset or will for His creation. God's soul is a consuming fire. "For our 'God is a consuming fire'" (Hebrews 12:29).

"Suddenly a sound like the blowing of a violent wind came from heaven and filled the whole house where they were sitting. They saw what seemed to be tongues of fire that separated and came to rest on each of them" (Acts 2:2–3). This describes the revealing of the Holy Spirit on the day of Pentecost. God's Spirit is the Holy Spirit. The spirit and the soul are interchangeable like the two sides of a coin. Both sides represent the same coin and have the same value.

It is necessary to understand that God is sensitive and His Spirit is pure, holy, and gentle, quick to love and forgive, and slow to anger and wrath. "And he passed in front of Moses, proclaiming, 'The Lord, the Lord, the compassionate and gracious God, slow to anger, abounding in love and faithfulness, maintaining love to thousands, and forgiving wickedness, rebellion and sin. Yet he does not leave the guilty unpunished; he punishes the children and their children for the sin of the fathers to the third and fourth generation'" (Exodus 34:6–7). God's Spirit is not hostile, anxious, or eager. He has great patience with man, life, and all His creation. Just as we can easily hear something or listen to it, God listens to our prayers and understands our hearts. In a similar way that we can see something or sincerely observe it, God notices our character and knows our spirits. He is able to bring us into maturity, as a bird does her children, feeding us easily in the beginning and building us up to fly out of the nest.

In seeing mankind and knowing that God, our Creator, is the reflection of our image, what He sees in the mirror, you may ponder on the existence of evil or where the female spirit of God dwells. The first thing we should realize is God's heart and perfect will for our creation in His body, the church. If we focus our attention on this, it will consume our finite minds and give us a simple perspective on how we should live. Yes, I can give a big theological understanding of evil, its existence, and how it affects our creation. However, when we direct our finite minds to God's plan for our salvation, we can realize that we are not meant to try to figure out God. It is not our problem to try to manage our creation. We need to humble ourselves to fit His perfect will. Nature holds a bundle of male and female characteristics. Life is good and gives us trials and lessons concerning good and evil. We are just creatures of this creation. It is not our place to concentrate on greater things.

Section 3: Opinion, Faith, and Beliefs

No matter what you read, or how well a book reads, you are experiencing beliefs based only on someone else's opinion. I am taking this fact into consideration as I write this book. The best way for me to illustrate this is through a lesson I learned during my freshman year at college. My English Comp. I and II teacher brought me through an obstacle course with my grades. She was known for assigning research papers that made up one-third to one-half of our semester grade. For the oddest reason, she kept giving me "Ds" and "Cs" on my research papers. Finally, after my third low grade, I asked her, "What am I doing wrong?" She told me that my research was based on the opinions of others. She wanted me to give my view on the assigned topics. This was a light to my dark conscience. She gave me an explanation that would last a lifetime. A thesis in a research paper is my personal opinion about the subject that I'm researching. This personal opinion becomes the focus of the whole composition.

Anything you read is based on the perspective of another person. Therefore, no matter how deep my writing gets, you can always find a counterpoint. As for your understanding of the philosophy I am expressing in *Wind ... Be Faithful to Me,* keep in mind that I am a philosopher. I have a bachelor's degree in communication and an associate's degree in culinary arts, which give me an authentic view on culture and religion. All the examples and ideas will be flavored by my background, environment, and personal testimony. Here is an illustration of my theories.

Is finding the right religion like following a recipe, or is it like a baking procedure in which you use a formula? When you use a recipe, you can add a little of something or take away something else. However, when you bake, you need to follow the formula exactly or the product will not come out right. If I were a legalist, I would say boldly that religion is like following a formula, but I'm not legalistic. Nevertheless, you do need to have an exact working belief system when coming to a relationship of understanding God. Otherwise, you will be lost. Since I'm not a legalist, I will boldly say that searching for the right concept comes from a pattern of learning and unlearning.

When you study how the Bible was written, your mind will be boggled as you consider the opinion and the mind of the one who put it together. Actually, when you think of how generic the Bible is in today's society (at least in the United States), it makes your head spin when you ponder how people took reality or their relationship of knowing God before the 1400s, before the first Bible was published. There is only so much information given in the Bible; however, if you focus on the heart of what God is relating to us, you can find a lifetime of knowledge to grow and learn from. As we see modern research documents, movies, and data on the subject of Jesus Christ, we find ourselves clueless on certain details of His life: His date of birth, His time of death, or why He used twelve disciples. The rest is left for our own interpretation for a reason.

Two principles pertain to God's method of granting our salvation: the law whereby those who live by the law are judged by the law, and the principle of grace. Regardless of our methods of belief, we are saved by grace. "For it is by grace you have been saved, through faith—and this not from yourselves, it is the gift of God—not by works, so that no one can boast" (Ephesians 2:8–9).

It is a matter of sin that is born in our nature that makes us self-destructive. Humbling ourselves to God's granted mercy reveals our hearts toward the Holy Spirit. The gift of salvation is granted to us by God's grace from our own faith so we can't boast on our salvation by our works. Seeing this fact in our hearts frees us from our responsibility to overcome sin and leaves the burden on our Savior, Jesus Christ. For by our own nature alone we are self-destructive, unable to manage the success of life or at least the success of salvation. This principle is the key to the moral understanding of the cross and the cornerstone to the glory of accepting Christianity. This very point is expressed by the Apostle Paul in Romans 7:21–25: "So I find this law at work: When I want to do good, evil is right there with me. For in my inner being I delight in God's law; but I see another law at work in the members of my body, waging war against the law of my mind and making me a prisoner of the law of sin at work within my members. What a wretched man I am! Who will rescue me from this body of death? Thanks be to God—through Jesus Christ our Lord!" Sin causes us all to fall short to the standards of God. Becoming spiritually sensitive to this principle is contradictory to the flesh but morally obligated to the spirit. Knowing that by our own nature we are destroyed brings us to the desire to seek relief. Answering all of our needs by His grace, God can become our craving and enter the emptiness in our lives.

Section 4: Salvation: A Concept or Reality

I have an expression that I like to use when I think of God calling His children from the world: "The church bells ring in every city." Even if the church bells are not preaching Christianity, they are still ringing. There still is a reason for mankind within society to turn to a God.

The reason you go to God is that you need Him; you need to be spiritually fed. If you do not thirst for God, you will not go to Him. You will become self-sufficient. The atheists' philosophy is that religion is a crutch for those who are weak and cannot comprehend the reality of mortality. However, the moral judgment and mentality needed to understand life after death are very sane. Coming to grips with a God or something to answer that big void of immorality and seeking eternal salvation are sobering to the human spirit. This very point of knowledge is healthy.

If there is one belief that I would like the reader to gain from this book, it is that living life by having a concept for salvation is a choice; not everyone in the world chooses to make this commitment.

By nature we are self-destructive; we need to come to grips of that to be sane. I'm not speaking about mental illness (although it does apply to that line of thinking); I'm speaking of the sanity of peace of mind—having a balance between your heart and mind, or being able to experience harmony between the physical world and the spiritual realm. The steps in accruing salvation come into reality only after you realize that you are not able to maintain balance alone. This is a life-long process; however, there is an absolute moment in one's life where it begins. Salvation or being saved is the process of growing in a relationship with God and going to heaven; regardless of your exact religious preference, seeing this point in life matters very dearly.

Question: What is salvation?

Answer: A concept of being saved.

The human spirit yearns toward God just as a plant feeds, yearns, and grows through sunlight. The behavior of a plant corresponds directly with its environment. The soil, water, temperature, and sunlight all affect the life and survival of a plant. Mother Nature nurtures a plant's life in a similar way to how God's Spirit nurtures the human spirit.

When someone thinks, "Gee, this act is hurting/destroying/damaging my relationship with God. I need to change," then that person is in touch with the reality of growth within his spirit. Just as a plant bends toward light, grows roots through soil for water, and moves within the relationship of its environment around it, the human heart feels the need of God's love. And just as a plant is depending on Mother Nature to provide its needs, the human soul relies on God's grace.

Salvation is a gift. "For it is by grace you have been saved, through faith—and this not from yourselves, it is the gift of God—not by works, so that no one can boast" (Ephesians 2:8–9). This gift is acquired only through faith and is not earned or deserved by anyone. This is another concept entirely concerning the subject. I spend at least one other section in this book on the topic of the grace of God, called "God's Mercy and Grace," but my effort on this massive topic is still quite shallow. The main point to realize is that it is all a matter of the heart. Having the attitude to read this book and gain the right perspective toward God is already showing a desire to obtain salvation. If you are beginning to yearn and are starting a relationship with God, then you are on the right track. Read Romans chapter 4 in the Bible for a better understanding of faith and how it applies to salvation. If you feel weird about reading the Bible, then read the section in this book called "The Bible: Face Value" in chapter 4. If you already have a strong relationship with God and are just looking for insight on having a more effective "Quiet Time," keep reading—the information and philosophies found in this book are good game for a religious appetite.

Chapter 2

Why Cry to the Father?

Section 1: Who Am I?

*W*ho is God? *What* does He say (or do)? *How* does He work His relationship and/or plan for our salvation? You may wonder why you should care. However, the humility of asking about the existence of God opens doors and brings us to the mouth of many rivers that flow to one body of water. What does this mean? Once you open your heart and set yourself on a journey of understanding this creation, coming from the Creator's perspective, He requires only one or a few beliefs for maintaining life.

We have a way of finding complete information for a story or an article in a newspaper or magazine. It is called the five "W's": "who," "what," "where," "when," and "why." (Actually, there is a sixth "W"—"which"—but we don't refer to this one for a report.) These five "W's," along with "how," give us a complete understanding of an idea expressed in an essay or story. If we answer the questions asked by these words, we cover most of the areas that are important to the audience. I am mentioning this concept because it follows the same format when it comes to understanding theology. However, there are only three questions related to this subject: "who," "what," and "how."

You see, God is powerful, wise, and loving, and His heart is to take care of us and carry us through life. A good illustration of this is found in a famous poem called "Footprints." The poem describes a man who finds God after his death. He asks Him an anxious question about why it seemed that God was not there in his life during the deepest, most sorrowful, and most painful moments. The answer to the man's question (to his surprise) was that God was carrying him through his deepest moments of pain. If you continue to read this book, I will go into deeper matters concerning the rationalization of following God. You may feel that I'm missing a very important part of this entire picture: "why." Why don't I answer the question, "Why does God allow things to happen the way they do?" Honestly, the most rigorous answer to this profound truth is simply this: "Because He wants to." The humility in accepting this answer as being the truth comes from experience.

The point of accepting God on His terms usually is the hardest thing for a new believer to do (as well as any devoted Christian). Why on God's terms, we ask? Why can't He come to me? Why does He allow so much pain to happen? What is God thinking about—doesn't He know that I'm confused? In understanding God's heart through the three questions of why, what, and how, the most important question to understand is "who."

"Wisdom is supreme; therefore get wisdom. Though it cost all you have, get understanding" (Proverbs 4:7). Finding faith is hard for a logical thinking person, yet finding faith is the most pleasing thing to God. "Now faith is being sure of what we hope for and certain of what we do not see. ... By faith we understand that the universe was formed at God's command, so that what is seen was not made out of what was visible. ... And without faith it is impossible to please God, because anyone who comes to him must believe that he exists and that he rewards those who earnestly seek him" (Hebrews 11:1, 3, 6).

One reason I can grasp the decision of believing in a personal, loving God so easily is because of the way my mother explained the creation to me when I was young. She said, "In the beginning there was God, and His Spirit moved across the face of the deep. And then God said to Himself, 'I'm lonely, so I'll create Myself a world so I can have man to worship Me.'" Now that I'm older, the idea that God was lonely and His purpose for the human race was for companionship seems very naïve, yet as a child I was able to grasp this message, and the door was open for me to swallow a deeper understanding of a loving, personal Father God.

God is a "who" with feelings, personality, character, a heart, and a mind. Most of the answers to why God does things a certain way is simply because He wants to, and finding the humility of accepting God on His terms brings us to a conclusion of no control.

Taking God at face value is the challenge of humans coming to an understanding of faith. If there is a God, and there is a place called heaven, and there is a plan for salvation, it might as well be the one God everyone accepts, who is good, loving, wise, and all-powerful. His plan for our salvation (if there is a plan) might as well be the plan that is easily accessible in the world or can be easily found and understood in a book or a map for life: the Bible. Why should we believe this? Because it is wise. Coming to an understanding of God on His terms is as hard as a decision. Not worrying about the things in life that we don't understand is wise. We did not have to understand life to become a part of it anyway. Believing that the Creator of all our lives and the Earth had a set plan and divine purpose for us that He wants us to understand is simply reasonable. Knowing this plan, what He says, and how He feels toward us (His creation) is simply accepting faith in God on His own terms. Accepting God on His own terms in the early stages of seeking a relationship with Him is very sagacious.

Section 2: Knowing How to Drop to Your Knees

Everybody has an experience of something I like to call "life hitting you in the face." It is inevitable just like puberty or old age. It is a part of life. How you react to this moment characterizes how you handle salvation. Some people turn to drugs or ego power—career, weightlifting, or sex—to either escape or feed the disease of having a life crisis. It may not have been one in the beginning, but a person's lack of a correct response causes an event to become a life crisis.

"From one man he made every nation of men, that they should inhabit the whole earth; and he determined the times set for them and the exact places where they should live. God did this so that men would seek him and perhaps reach out for him and find him, though he is not far from each one of us" (Acts 17:26–27).

Why should we consider God's divine plan for our lives? What makes that path correct and all other paths wrong? What is the track record of evidence of God's love in your life? Until you find answers to these questions, faith in God and all the fellowship and religion that come with it do not really add up to a wise path. Ironically, it is because of these crises or the mysteriousness of fate that God's pathway makes all the sense in the world. However, much like pregnancy, marriage, and parenthood, until you personally experience God's plan, you are left in the dark about the results.

Some people will not accept God's name or word until He proves to pass their finite knowledge or beliefs. "We should not test the Lord, as some of them did—and were killed by snakes" (1 Corinthians 10:9). Jesus said to Satan, "It says: 'Do not put the Lord your God to the test'" (Luke 4:12).

In today's modern society, we turn to sexual relationships, counseling, medication, psychiatrists, and other outside influences to feed our starving spirits. Nevertheless, even doctors, psychiatrists, nurses, and counselors have found it empty to put all their trust in the medical profession. There is a new wave movement in which the mind, body, and spirit are considered equally important in good human health. Research on laughter, forgiveness, and positive thinking (or faith) has become the professionals' answers for many medical problems. Finding a balance between body and spirit and believing in it as a course of life and purpose are rewarding accomplishments.

Death in the family, serious accidents, being incarcerated, or being hospitalized for a medical reason such as a major illness are some of the crises in life that humble our spirits and bring us to a breaking point in our mentality. We all have spiritual dilemmas that cause us to question the spiritual realm and the physical control we have in life. It may not always be obvious; it can be obscure.

During a performance by the famous comedian Richard Pryor, he explained a shocking revelation that changed his life. While taking a vacation in Africa, he noticed the dominance of black culture and felt a genuine connection with his roots from the motherland. As his vacation ended and he prepared to come home, he looked at the culture of an African city at the airport and came to a powerful conclusion. "Did you see any 'niggers' here while you were in Africa?" he asked himself. To his surprise, the answer was no. He even realized that the word never entered his mind the entire vacation. From that moment forward, this man who made millions of dollars mocking the Afro-American culture by saying "nigger," causing both black and white audiences to laugh, decided to never say "nigger" again.

It can be just that sedating, or it can be shocking. We learn about God through family, from other believers witnessing to us, or even from understanding our own culture and society. But until we hit that point of reality and we are broken down to our knees, it never really makes sense to us.

Knowing when to drop to your knees is the beginning of understanding faith and believing in God. Some people witness a miracle after having a "bathroom prayer." Some see the light after observing the miracles happening in other people's lives. There is nothing left to say; coming to a spiritual crossroad in life is inevitable, and we all will in our own time. Accepting faith in God and finding His purpose in your life are miracle solutions to life's problems. The truth is that God wants us all to seek Him and find His heart in our lives; however, people have their own free will and can choose whatever they like to deal with life's spiritual realm. One day you open your eyes and realize that you are going to die. You already knew that, but one day you sober up and realize it differently. Where you stand at judgment when you finally do die is all determined by that turning point.

Section 3: God's Mercy and Grace

My biological brother, Clifford, was giving me some of his spiritual insight. He based his insight from a passage in the Bible: "But you, brothers, are not in darkness so that this day should surprise you like a thief. You are all sons of the light and sons of the day. We do not belong to the night or to the darkness. So then, let us not be like others, who are asleep, but let us be alert and self-controlled. For those who sleep, sleep at night, and those who get drunk, get drunk at night. But since we belong to the day, let us be self-controlled, putting on faith and love as a breastplate, and the hope of salvation as a helmet. For God did not appoint us to suffer wrath but to receive salvation through our Lord Jesus Christ. He died for us so that, whether we are awake or asleep, we may live together with him. Therefore encourage one another and build each other up, just as in fact you are doing" (1 Thessalonians 5:4–11). My brother does not believe that God's children were meant to be overly active at night. He feels that the nighttime is for drunks, prostitutes, and others involved in foolish worldly living. He says, "We are of the light," meaning "daylight."

Indifferent to how wise and profound this attitude in life may appear, many believers do not follow this nature of conduct. This way of thinking may be right, or it may be wrong, but what matters most is that one believes in this manner of thinking. Therefore, if one believes in this way of living, he will be judged based on his conduct. The perspective you are living by holds only a very small amount of light that is given in life. It is like starlight. Although the stars light up the night, one star, regardless of the enormous power it radiates, is very minute in comparison to the size of the universe. The understanding we have to guide our lives is defective within our own mentality. Yes, my brother is basing his belief from the Bible; nevertheless, the measurement of judgment for his salvation is still greater than his personal opinion from the Bible.

Realizing that we do not have all the answers in life is moralized; however, even after using the wisest strategy, we still may be wrong. Yet, coming to the rationalization that we need help has a high amount of prestige. We behave and form our character by a belief system. Our personal belief system forms our mentality; by nature, our mentality is self-destructive. This is why we need a "higher power" or spiritual structure to guide us. You may not want to agree on the morals of having Jesus Christ in your life, but do you feel that you can acquire the means of salvation alone? There is something sobering in understanding that you cannot manage on your own. My brother says, "We are born into the light." Then he expands his concept into believing our physical bodies shut down at night. This depth in his beliefs allows him to feel secure about his own spirit. He feels as if he is relying on God; for this very reason, I respect his judgment.

Section 4: Into His Hands

Separating God's heart from His plan of salvation is like separating the wind from the movement of the trees. First there is a will and then there is a reaction. We, as humans, maintain a hunger and thirst for God's spirit, whether we comprehend this reality or not. Living in the body with likeminded believers helps our spirits remain active or "on fire." No one can manage to save one's soul alone. The church is God's plan for mankind, not ours. Our own lives have fallen through our hands into the hands of God. This in itself is a good thing, although some people have difficulty accepting the lack of power. The fate of our lives falls through our hands because we do not understand.

One could have an understanding of a trade or knowledge of a special career, but not earn a salary equal to his skills. On the other hand, one could have a good understanding of managing money and have business skills that cause him to make a high standard of living without having the education or extensive training in one skill. You do not need training or education of a skill or trade if you have the ability to make a living from having business and financial understanding. Likewise, you do not need religion, church, or theology if you have a humble heart and a compatible relation within your heart and spirit. Your lifestyle will be the evidence of your salvation. You can have all the knowledge of religion and theology, yet not contain the proper spirit to sustain salvation. Naturally, our spirits yearn for the Holy Spirit. "In the same way, the Spirit helps us in our weakness. We do not know what we ought to pray for, but the Spirit himself intercedes for us with groans that words cannot express" (Romans 8:26).

Yet, by our own nature we cannot find the comfort of God's spirit. This is why His word, through the Bible and the church, tells us how to comprehend a pathway and find a workable course of action for salvation in our lives. Some people find a suitable course in life that does not consider the means of God and spirituality or religion; nevertheless, those people who have found peace with God and satisfaction in the testimony of Jesus Christ know that walking the pathway of life without God is foolish. What really matters? As a like-minded Christian believer, I express the Word of God as evidence of what pathway to follow in life. I did not put this creation into existence from before I was born. Why should I feel as if I have overcome this existence of life now? What does God's Word say about me as a man, my power and ability to find satisfaction on my own, or my skills to earn my own salvation?

> This righteousness from God comes through faith in Jesus Christ to all who believe. There is no difference, for all have sinned and fall short of the glory of God. (Romans 3:22–23)

> When he [the Holy Spirit] comes, he will convict the world of guilt in regard to sin and righteousness and judgment: in regard to sin, because men do not believe in me; in regard to righteousness, because I am going to the Father, where you can see me no longer; and in regard to judgment, because the prince of this world now stands condemned. (John 16:8–11)

> Jesus said, "If you [the Pharisees] were blind, you would not be guilty of sin; but now that you claim you can see, your guilt remains." (John 9:41)

> If we claim to be without sin, we deceive ourselves and the truth is not in us. If we confess our sins, he is faithful and just and will forgive us our sins and purify us from all unrighteousness. If we claim we have not sinned, we make him out to be a liar and his word has no place in our lives. (1 John 1:8–10)

Why should we care about what God's Word says? For one reason: it is wise. If we did not know how to swim and found ourselves surrounded by deep waters, someone throwing us a life raft could save us from our despair. But we must realize that we are drowning before we can see the reasoning of being saved. God made us. He took the time to create our bodies with His own hands, and in the palm of His hands lie the plan of our salvation. "Can a mother forget the baby at her breast and have no compassion on the child she has borne? Though she may forget, I will not forget you!

See, I have engraved you on the palms of my hands; your walls are ever before me" (Isaiah 49:15–16).

Why would God have the knowledge and power to create the skies, water, air, trees, and humans, and not have the desire or will to care and nurture His creation? God is love. We are His creation, and He created us with His love. Our lives should rest in His hands, for it is better than anything else.

Faith may be a hard concept to comprehend; our hearts are beyond our own grasp of education, and no one can figure it out. The topic of salvation may be too much to swallow, but the simplicity of having a little humility to allow your life to fall from your hands into the hands of God is sagacious. And God's capacity to handle the task is evidently as accurate as mathematical logic or the laws of physics.

Chapter 3

Evangelism, Witnessing, and Testimonies

"From one man he made every nation of men, that they should inhabit the whole earth; and he determined the times set for them and the exact places where they should live. God did this so that men would seek him and perhaps reach out for him and find him, though he is not far from each one of us" (Acts 17:26–27).

Perhaps you still feel a little alienated with this book, and you are still not sure how it applies to you or where you fit into the whole picture. In every city the church bell rings; we all have a part in God's plan. Although you may have never attended a church service, you hear the Word of God calling in the wind, and it is your responsibility to respond. I am going to describe eight characters in a play called "Life" that I have encountered and watched how they made an impact on my evangelism. All these characters are real, and their lives have grown and possibly changed since this book was published. Try to relate to each or even one of them either personally or by association. Their names have been changed to protect their legal rights of privacy.

The first character is Edna. She is what you might consider part of the church's "fashion." She has attended church for most of her life, although she has often fallen from fellowship. She is easily influenced by people's (stranger's) opinions, and she does not have a strong "backbone." She is constantly searching for a church home. Jesus speaks of her in His "Parable of the Sower" found in Luke chapter 8. She was a seed that fell along the path: "It was trampled on, and the birds of the air ate it up." I have met this woman in my home church. She does not attend our church anymore; however, she does attend another one. She was considered "one who fell through the cracks of the system." She reminds me of how my father describes elderly black churchwomen seen every Sunday waving their fans—somewhat like Aunt Esther on the television show *Sanford and Son*.

God comes into our lives in several different ways. Meet my other friend Beth. She considers herself a Jew by birth. She was raised in a Jewish family. She often mocked Christianity and despised the teachings of her Christian friends, even though she constantly hung around them. The people you associate with play a big part in building your character and in how God calls you out of the world. "Do not envy wicked men, do not desire their company; for their hearts plot violence, and their lips talk about making trouble" (Proverbs 24:1–2). "Do not be misled: 'Bad company corrupts good character'" (1 Corinthians 15:33). Eventually Beth got baptized, and she currently is in fellowship at a local church in her community.

Our next character is Bruce. He is an associate. I became acquainted with him through a mutual friend named Robert. He also associates with Christian believers, yet he never felt comfortable around Christian traditions. He felt out of place at weddings and church services. He also glamorized women and lived impurely and immorally with his girlfriends. Currently he is one who likes to play in the playground of worldliness and not guard his heart. Ironically, our mutual friend Robert is a fire-breathing, Bible-talking disciple who was called out of a biological family of unbelievers. It is obvious that Bruce is very attracted to the light of Christ. I pray that his associates will convert him into a Christian.

James, our next character, called himself an agnostic. He became a very close friend of mine while I attended college and was president of the philosophy club. James was very confused about religion; nevertheless, he had a good understanding of the spiritual realm. Because his seed was in bad soil (rebellious nature), his spirit could not grow. Jesus describes four seeds in his "Parable of the Sower" in Luke 8. James is another example of the seed that fell along the path: "Those along the path are the ones who hear, and then the devil comes and takes away the word from their hearts, so that they may not believe and be saved." This character illustrates how the light of Christ can shine through in some souls and uncover darkness in others. Sunlight can melt butter, but it can also harden clay.

Lucy, our fifth character, became my associate through a more recent friend named Weezer. She has a weak attraction to the light. She admires her Christian friends but lives an impure and unholy life. She indulged in alcohol and has immoral relationships. This results in weak faith. She writes about her misery in poetry and reads them in local bars and coffee shops. Satan has a way of making a cartoon out of life and trapping people in a mockery of God's Word. Lucy is trapped in society's web of wickedness. A good Bible verse to describe her lifestyle is in Luke 21:34: "Be careful, or your hearts will be weighed down with dissipation, drunkenness and the anxieties of life, and that day will close on you unexpectedly like a trap."

Our next character is Maria. She is a true illustration of my expression: "The church bell rings every Sunday"; she hears her calling. She is a young, attractive lady who works at the local liquor store. She mentioned to my mother that she wanted to go to church, so I reached out to her. I invited her to a service, but circumstances kept coming up so she never made it. However, she did join another church, her grandmother's, near her house. She has not been baptized yet, and she has a husband who does not want anything to do with church. Jesus gives an example of her character when he says, "Other seed fell among thorns, which grew up with it and choked the plants. ... The seed that fell among thorns stands for those who hear, but as they go on their way they are choked by life's worries, riches and pleasures, and they do not mature." Maria is currently considering divorce.

In every story there is an adversary, and in this play of "Life" we have Tiffany. She is a bad seed. She believes that she is smarter than the Bible because of her research and study on the subject. Tiffany does not have any respect for Jesus or the cross. She considers herself a good person because she does not do drugs and believes in saving the Earth. She protests constantly. She pushes her lifestyle onto her children, and they are growing to be just like her. We all have choices in life. Robert came from a non-believing family, and he turned his life to Christ. Through Tiffany I can see why God of the Old Testament would destroy entire families because of the sins of their fathers.

This prepares the entrance of our last character; we will call him John Doe. I called Tiffany the adversary, but John Doe is just foolish. "The fool says in his heart, 'There is no God.' They are corrupt, their deeds are vile; there is no one who does good" (Psalm 14:1). I met John Doe one night after a concert at a local diner. John does not believe in God. He does not believe that it makes any sense. He says it cannot be true. He feels that religious people are afraid of their immortality and that he is strong by accepting his end, which is death. He does not believe in a Virgin Mary birth, yet does accept the reality of a virgin birth. He said that during the

Civil War a bullet was fired and went through a Confederate soldier's genital into the womb of a woman who was directly behind him. The bullet carried the soldier's semen, which caused the woman to get pregnant. She was a virgin!

Hopefully, you do not see yourself in the subjects described so far. These characters are real, and they are acting out salvation in real life. The sobering truth about their stories is that you can't act out the course of salvation. Just as blood is real, there is a direct purpose for every human. As powerful as sunlight is, there is a corresponding meaning in life. In the same way that God breathed into plants through sunlight (photosynthesis) and established a set plan for seeds, He established His kingdom. In His kingdom we have a place to belong, and the blessing of salvation is given to us all to fulfill in our lives.

Part 2

The Relationship

Chapter 4

His Spirit in the Wind

Section 1: Religions in the World

When someone approaches you talking about religion, you may have feelings of distrust and discomfort toward that person. What is the right response? How should I respect what the Word of God says? "Anyone who listens to the word but does not do what it says is like a man who looks at his face in a mirror and, after looking at himself, goes away and immediately forgets what he looks like. But the man who looks intently into the perfect law that gives freedom, and continues to do this, not forgetting what he has heard, but doing it—he will be blessed in what he does" (James 1:23–25).

The Methodist preaches about the sinner's prayer (Romans 10:9–10). The Pentecostal spreads the news of speaking in tongues as the evidence of receiving the Holy Spirit. The Catholic talks about Purgatory and honors infant baptism. We may hear someone tell us that our baptism was not valid or you cannot have more than one baptism, or after you are saved you can still lose your salvation (Ephesians 2:8–9).

What is the heart of the matter?

Do you seem to have the view in your mind of racing aimlessly to an end of some sort of convicting death? That is very scary. Jesus is the answer. If I were to put nails in my palms and feet and hang high on some hill waiting for some torturous, agonizing death to show you this point, you still may disbelieve the matter. Therefore, why should I speak of it? What is actually more revealing is what God says to be true. There is an expression I use in my mind while I am contemplating life: "Everybody has to answer to his own tombstone." The fact that you may have some convictions in life and still be living a lie is very much reality. If you feel in your soul that Jesus is the answer and you are just trying to find a way to make His testimony work, then you are missing the objective. Religion is based on a philosophical understanding, and this philosophy forms a lifestyle of understanding the heart behind religion and not allowing it to become a legalistic science. You may trust your heart, but you do not have to understand it.

For the remainder of this book, I am going to base all my religious knowledge and philosophy on Christianity. Honestly, if you cannot come to a rationalization with this in your heart now, you need to put this book down. Because I have to answer to my own tombstone the meaning of Christianity, I need to evangelize.

"Son of man, speak to your countrymen and say to them: 'When I bring the sword against a land, and the people of the land choose one of their men and make him their watchman, and he sees the sword coming against the land and blows the trumpet to warn the people, then if anyone hears the trumpet but does not take warning and the sword comes and takes his life, his blood will be on his own head. Since he heard the sound of the trumpet but did not take warning, his blood will be on his own head. If he had taken warning, he would have saved himself. But if the watchman sees the sword coming and does not blow the trumpet to warn the people and the sword comes and takes the life of one of them, that man will be taken away because of his sin, but I will hold the watchman accountable for his blood'" (Ezekiel 33:2–6).

I am just standing in the battle.

Section 2: The Bible: Face Value

God communicates differently with man today than He did in the times of the Old Testament, both socially and personally. In the Old Testament, He spoke through prophets, apostles, and godly men and women of leadership such as David, Abraham, and Noah. He spoke directly with His voice to men through their ears. They could understand Him from clouds, fire, and elements. Now He speaks spirit to spirit, revealing Himself in our hearts through His Holy Spirit. Now we speak to God directly; each man and woman can pray to reach God's ears and heart without the mediation of priesthood.

This all became possible through His Son, Jesus. Jesus was a prophet, a Messiah, and a Savior. He communicated face to face with men and women when He walked the Earth. He took away the separation from man through His death. The mediation of priesthood was gone, for He tore the veil (Luke 23:44–46). We can now communicate to God directly spirit to spirit, face to Jesus' face.

In the beginning, Adam and Eve were able to talk to God directly, face to face, spirit to God, but this method of communication was broken by the disobedience of Adam and Eve and the creation of sin. Everything was created by God, and God is good. Because God is good and He created everything, everything from origin is good. God did not create bad. The creation God created had the ability to create. Through the creation's ability create, bad was created. God did not destroy evil. He destroyed the world and all of mankind except one family, but He did not destroy evil. He could have destroyed evil. It would be logical to believe that because of God's infinite knowledge, He saw a purpose in evil. He saw how evil could be used for His good.

Years ago, while I was earning my associate's degree in Fort Wayne, Indiana, I fellowshipped and became acquainted with two of my favorite cousins, Shawn and Gail. Gail had an expression that stuck with me for years. She would look at an issue, and as she judged the facts in whatever circumstances she was observing, she would say, "Well, that is just the lesser of two evils." This is somewhat like a teenage female being impregnated by an adult male. You could call the man a child molester and lock him up for life, yet light and love are found in the moral of the circumstances: the girl and her family now are blessed with a new child in the world.

This is how I view using the Bible to understand how God communicates through life. One could say it is manmade, butchered by different preachers, wrongly interpreted, and biased when translated by the church and spiritual scholars of our time. However, the fact that a pure and holy God who is personal, with heart feelings and a conscience, sees it fit and wise to give a book of instructions on how to understand life's morals and lessons, which helps us to complete life's journey successfully, is good. It is the lesser of two evils to accept the flaws of a manmade historical document and to embrace the love, unity, and spiritual wisdom found in the Bible.

I use the Bible to find spiritual knowledge and have faith in God to believe He understands my heart and desire to serve Him. Faith is like yeast—a little amount can be incorporated in a lot of life when it is alive and active. Taking the Bible at face value to interpret life's lessons and morals is very practical.

The Bible in its English translation is only five hundred years old, yet it is like fibers within our daily culture. Shakespeare's plays are older than the publication of the Bible. What we remember of Romeo and Juliet, Michelangelo's paintings, and Beethoven's Fifth Symphony have the same history date as the English translation of the books of the Bible. It is not that the writing did not exist, but we take the facts in it as reference like dictionaries or encyclopedias, and anyone can have access to it in America. Any child today with a healthy look at Christianity and a good understanding of a library can find the path to salvation.

You may consider my beliefs wrong, narrow, or biased; nevertheless, they are still my beliefs. They form my conscience; therefore, I have an attitude and a heart that what I understand about religion is true. It was once said by an anonymous speaker that what one finds to be true in his or her heart to be true for all mankind is a sin of sheer genius. Thus, when approaching the subject of religion, if people base their knowledge or testimony on their hearts, they will find a universal voice.

Section 3: Christianity

When you look at religions in the world, three of them dominate the entire spectrum: Judaism, Islam, and Christianity. All three follow history through the Bible and believe in worshiping one God, for the most part the same God: Jesus' Father, the great I Am, Jehovah. What is the difference in what all these religions believe? Which one reflects the most important part of how humankind sees the heart of the Word? To get a better answer to these questions, I feel it is better to ask first why there is a division.

I think that God allows a division of religions both within Christianity and outside in other religions for the same reason that He divided the languages at the Tower of Babel. It is a perspective for humans to see a matter of humility. When God put division in the tongue, He knew that society would still find a way to build a civilization; however, their focus for a culture would be different. Whether or not they understood the reason that God did what He did, they knew that building the tower was wrong. God is in control. Why we need to understand a main perception to live our lives is irrelevant. Although we may be able to discern the difference between right and wrong, we have no insight to make final moral judgments. Humans do not need to understand.

A good illustration of how God governs the world is in His Word on slavery. He does not say that slavery is a sin. There is no commandment that says, "Thou shalt not answer to another human." He does command humans not to lie, yet He says that humans should love their slave masters and work sincerely for them. What is God's heart on the matter? He led Israel (His chosen people) from Egypt and out of captivity. Did He do this to show grace for His own name's sake? Regardless of the answer, we still saw the reality of His will for humans. Understanding God's grace and doing His will are more important than trying to grasp the knowledge of why we need to obey. You do not understand God's will until you obey it. God allows His will to be spoken through war, yet he told His beloved servant David while he was king that since he spilled much blood during his life, he wouldn't be allowed to build the holy temple of God. The temple was built during the reign of David's son Solomon. Again we see God's action, but do we understand His heart?

How should we view religion in the world and what it says? It is my opinion that I am not to preach what it says; I believe it is more important to respect and do what it says. Although Islam, Judaism, and Christianity are preaching different things, they all go back to the basic ethic of God's nature. Judaism is to Christianity as Latin is to the English language. Both Islam and Judaism rebuke the testimony of Jesus Christ. Islam brings its history back to God's chosen people of Israel without the redemption and reconciliation of humans through Jesus Christ, which is justified in history. Judaism does not accept the changes in the stars, the calendar, or the doctrine that A.D. Christianity has a relationship with the Father. Islam holds the bloodline of the chosen people of God but does not honor a plan of salvation and redemption of sin. Judaism continues to worship God without accepting the holy anointing of the Holy Spirit.

All good, moral people who try to obey the rules of God's plan of salvation, but have no heart to love the Word of God who created them, miss the mark of harmony and balance between themselves and God. God wants our hearts. Having the knowledge of God and wisdom of His doctrine without the passion for the Scriptures is calamity. "If I speak in the tongues of men and of angels, but have not love, I am only a resounding gong or a clanging cymbal" (1 Corinthians 13:1). Christianity gives us a relationship with God so we can embrace His heart. He gave us free will so we do not worship as robots, and He gives us His Son so we do not serve resentfully.

The best approach to having daily spiritual devotions to God is to first come to a clear focus of who God is, what He says, and why we should worship Him. Although there are other religions in the world besides Christianity, the story of Jesus and the effect of His life best reflect the heart of God. Understanding the relationship with the Creator will humble your heart to serve, and even better, gain a stronger desire to worship Him.

Chapter 5

The Plan

Section 1: The Cross

In this section of the book, I plan to explain the basic testimony of any Christian who has found freedom from sin and redemption through God's Son and our Savior Jesus Christ. Many people feel that this is the most important part of the book. I am not sure if I agree. My heart was not to preach the common slogan that has attracted so many Christian denominations; however, I wanted to express the important points of love and theological understanding that are so easily missed when someone tries to accept the concept of having a stronger relationship with God. Although I may not consider this section the most important, I do feel that the words of the Apostle Paul best explain the importance of the history concerning God's Son on the cross and how it changed the face of history and our relationship as humankind with God. Therefore, I will explain through the Bible:

> Therefore, just as sin entered the world through one man, and death through sin, and

in this way death came to all men, because all sinned—for before the law was given, sin was in the world. But sin is not taken into account when there is no law. Nevertheless, death reigned from the time of Adam to the time of Moses, even over those who did not sin by breaking a command, as did Adam, who was a pattern of the one to come.

But the gift is not like the trespass. For if the many died by the trespass of the one man, how much more did God's grace and the gift that came by the grace of the one man, Jesus Christ, overflow to the many! Again, the gift of God is not like the result of the one man's sin: The judgment followed one sin and brought condemnation, but the gift followed many trespasses and brought justification. For if, by the trespass of the one man, death reigned through that one man, how much more will those who receive God's abundant provision of grace and of the gift of righteousness reign in life through the one man, Jesus Christ.

Consequently, just as the result of one trespass was condemnation for all men, so also the result of one act of righteousness was justification that brings life for all men. For just as through the disobedience of the one man the many were made sinners, so also through the obedience of the one man the many will be made righteous.

The law was added so that the trespass might increase. But where sin increased, grace increased all the more, so that, just as sin reigned in death, so also grace might reign through righteousness to bring eternal life through Jesus Christ our Lord.

What shall we say, then? Shall we go on sinning so that grace may increase? By no means! We died to sin; how can we live in it any longer? Or don't you know that all of us who were baptized into Christ Jesus were baptized into his death? We were therefore buried with him through baptism into death in order that, just as Christ was raised from the dead through the glory of the Father, we too may live a new life.

If we have been united with him like this in his death, we will certainly also be united with him in his resurrection. For we know that our old self was crucified with him so that the body of sin might be done away with, that we should no longer be slaves to sin—because anyone who has died has been freed from sin.

Now if we died with Christ, we believe that we will also live with him. For we know that since Christ was raised from the dead, he cannot die again; death no longer has mastery over him. The death he died, he died to sin once for all; but the life he lives, he lives to God.

In the same way, count yourselves dead to sin but alive to God in Christ Jesus. Therefore do not let sin reign in your mortal body so that you obey its evil desires. Do not offer the parts of your body to sin, as instruments of wickedness, but rather offer yourselves to God, as those who have been brought from death to life; and offer the parts of your body

> to him as instruments of righteousness. For sin shall not be your master, because you are not under law, but under grace. (Romans 5:12–6:14)

The exact nature of what is tempting for me as a writer and philosopher I will purposely avoid. I would normally rewrite and summarize the passage I just quoted from the Apostle Paul. Normally I try to better explain the passage so that I would feel that you would understand it. However, by doing this, I would undo the task I wanted to illustrate by using Paul's words instead of mine. I do not want to explain the testimony of the cross through my personal experience or opinion, and I also want to let the Word of God in the Bible speak for itself. However, I will leave you with a thought to ponder: consider the idea that God gave His Son to humankind to die on the cross. We humans forgot and disregarded remembering and celebrating the life and testimony of Jesus Christ through Christmas, Easter, and the A.D. calendar. It would stand to reason that this act of nature through humankind would anger and disappoint our Lord to make Him destroy all humans and the world would end. Nevertheless, God saw that man would grasp the concept of His plan for salvation through Jesus Christ our Lord, revealing the heart of God in this world throughout our social structure and lifestyle. Reflecting the soul of Christ, we can see God's bride, the church, and the Holy Spirit surrounding God's very Word. God's soul is a consuming fire.

Section 2: Our Nature, Our Sins

For the life of me, I do not see why God did not allow my character to be disciplined through the rigorous environment of the U.S. military force. At this point in my life, it is definite that I will not be drafted or allowed in the Armed Forces through voluntary actions. Three times while I was a teenager, I attempted to join the service. For reasons not out of my control but directly due to my sins, I was not allowed.

The reason I question this fact in my life is because of one area of my character that has always caused a weakness in my spiritual development: discipline. As a teenager, I was extremely rebellious. I became aware as a young adult that I was what you would call a prodigal child. It was due to drugs and incarceration that I was not allowed to join the military, and that I did not pass the military exam.

Why would I bring up this matter in my personal development? It is because at a very young age I was also called by God to serve in His army and ministry. I rebelled against this calling; nevertheless, I was significantly called. "So I find this law at work: When I want to do good, evil is right there with me. For in my inner being I delight in God's law; but I see another law at work in the members of my body, waging war against the law of my mind and making me a prisoner of the law of sin at work within my members. What a wretched man I am! Who will rescue me from this body of death? Thanks be to God—through Jesus Christ our Lord!" (Romans 7:21–25).

Becoming a Christian is not a matter of saying (or praying) a few words or being immersed in a body of water; you have to behave a certain way to be accepted as God's child. You are not required to have devotions with God every day. However, you do need to have devotions religiously or in some manner of discipline. Having a hunger for God should come naturally to your spirit, like plants hungering for sunlight. You should not allow your spirit to thirst but maintain a balance in your mind and heart to remain in harmony with the spirit of the Lord. An unbalanced soul will not remain in God's spirit. Discipline is something I have learned from the school of hard knocks. Even though I may not carry the common lifestyle of an evangelist or prophet, one thing I do greatly understand and desire in my relationship with God is His grace.

Do not get the impression that I am against "daily quiet times" or the disciplined action it takes to make it your habit. In a matter of consideration, I am definitely for early morning daily devotions. I know that it is an effective way to make God your priority. However, I also know that God will meet your heart wherever you are, and the lack of discipline in your life should not hinder your ability of being saved. The most important thing to remember is that spirituality does not come naturally. It is human nature to sin. Realizing this important fact and taking a sobering look at your soul will give you deep insight into where you are spiritually with God. The urgency for salvation should come at a point of balance and harmony between your heart and mind. Only then will a door open, and you will find guidance in what you must do to be right with God.

Section 3: In Conclusion

"Now all has been heard; here is the conclusion of the matter: Fear God and keep his commandments, for this is the whole duty of man. For God will bring every deed into judgment, including every hidden thing, whether it is good or evil" (Ecclesiastes 12:13–14).

In conclusion to the matter, sometimes the wind blows and the chill touches your bones and lets you know that you are alive. Knowledge carries great respect when it is understood. Do you believe this summary of knowledge from the great and wisest man of the world, King Solomon? Does it send chills up your spine? Do you believe that one day you are going to be judged?

In my life I have experienced faith in two ways: aimlessly chasing after the wind like a madman in anxiety and fear, and dancing within it gracefully as I hear my name being called repeatedly like a song. Loving God is easy. Understanding love is hard. A lifetime of work could not equal the complete comprehension of love, yet it is the only thing in life that actually matters. Although King Solomon actually found a conclusion to the matters of life before he found his entire life ending, he still allowed a great deal of knowledge to be open to a vast empty space left in the hours and days in his life. "As for man, his days are like grass, he flourishes like a flower of the field; the wind blows over it and it is gone, and its place remembers it no more" (Psalm 103:15–16).

Our quiet times spent with God are part of our personal spiritual discipline as well as social obligation toward the rest of the body, the church of Christ. Everybody's happiness is personal. God wants us to be happy and tells us how to be happy, and God's character is revealed in His Word, the Bible. Only through effective "quiet times" can God open your heart (eyes) to express His love for you and for your brothers and sisters in Christ. It also helps you guard your heart against the subtle, cunning schemes of the adversary. We cannot expect to grasp and understand and complete the plan of salvation and our happiness on our own. It is a relationship with our God through His Son Jesus Christ that opens the door of redemption. "Trust in the Lord with all your heart and lean not on your own understanding; in all your ways acknowledge him, and he will make your paths straight" (Proverbs 3:5–6).

Part 3

Practical

Chapter 6

Seven Steps of Wisdom

In the process of writing a book on "quiet times" or "daily devotions," you'll picture either one or two concepts: a book on daily reflections with Scripture verses to accommodate, or a positive expression book referring to wise phrases or thoughts to reflect on. In reading this book you might have thought, "Wow, where is he going with these thoughts on theology?" Believe me when I say that I understand why this style of a "devotional handbook" is rather unusual. However, I wanted to grasp the entire aspect of God (which isn't possible) and allow you as a reader to view your heart on religion. This chapter is probably the closest to what you would look for in a handbook on daily devotions. It still does not give you daily scriptures or wise phrases reflecting spirituality, but it does help you embrace the meaning of a Christian's quiet time. This chapter explores seven personal habits you should obtain to be a mature, growing Christian.

Above all of the practices, the most important is prayer. In every relationship (consider marriage), communication is the key to growth. Prayer is how you communicate with God. It is not so much how you pray, but what you believe while you are praying and how your faith builds as you focus on the one you are praying to. I explain six other practices that are key to a growing spiritual lifestyle: reading Scriptures, fellowship, fasting, writing, singing, and tithing. Yet, if you find yourself desperate to apply your heart to a spiritual principle, you can start with prayer. You can even begin to pray right now. No experience is required for this principle to work.

"But when he asks, he must believe and not doubt, because he who doubts is like a wave of the sea, blown and tossed by the wind" (James 1:6).

"And without faith it is impossible to please God, because anyone who comes to him must believe that he exists and that he rewards those who earnestly seek him" (Hebrews 11:6).

Section 1: Praying

As I start to explore the seven practices that a Christian should embrace to mature spiritually, I give great emphasis on prayer. What is prayer? It is a telephone call to God, an e-mail chat with Jesus, an open-heart romance dialogue with the Holy Spirit, an honest heart-to-heart talk with a friend, and a real down-to-earth confession to someone who knows all about you already but still wishes to hear the words coming from your lips. It is because a sincere attitude is so important when you approach this habit that I first opened the book with a view of who God is: a personal, living spirit with a heart, feelings, and emotions. The institution of marriage is probably the best example of how this relationship should be established. Although not everyone who prays is married or has a successful marriage, God's bride, the Church, has an interpersonal experience with her spouse, Jesus. Nevertheless, believing in an ultimate Spirit who actually cares for you and wants to establish a central loving relationship with you is the most valuable point. In believing this, you will understand in your heart and mind to live by faith, a faith that will never fail, leave, or deceive you.

Section 2: Reading Scriptures

There is a deadly spiritual disease that infects many people and excludes the principle of humility. It agrees with the very sin of the devil, which is pride in the heart. "How you have fallen from heaven, O morning star, son of the dawn! You have been cast down to the earth, you who once laid low the nations! You said in your heart, 'I will ascend to heaven; I will raise my throne above the stars of God; I will sit enthroned on the mount of assembly, on the utmost heights of the sacred mountain. I will ascend above the tops of the clouds; I will make myself like the Most High.' But you are brought down to the grave, to the depths of the pit" (Isaiah 14:12–15).

This disease is not a matter of ethical pride or a mental attitude of confidence that causes you to strive for excellence for God in all you do in your job, home, and community. Rather, it is a selfish, arrogant pride. The sinful disease is a belief that you are smarter than the Bible. "He mocks proud mockers but gives grace to the humble" (Proverbs 3:34). Many people go out of their way to research different religions and consider other avenues of salvation (definition: delivery from their sins) outside of Christianity or what is explained in the Bible. I myself confess to doing this in my past. You would think to yourself, "Salvation. Wow—that is a big subject. I need to make sure that I'm right." However, it is that exact reason that simplicity is so wise. "The law of the Lord is perfect, reviving the soul. The statutes of the Lord are trustworthy, making wise the simple" (Psalm 19:7). "Your statutes are wonderful; therefore I obey them. The unfolding of your words gives light; it gives understanding to the simple" (Psalm 119:129–130).

Why wouldn't God present the recipe for success in life and all the ingredients of His Word in a simple book that we can all read for our own salvation? But you may think that everybody in the world is not associated with the Bible or Christianity. And that is my exact point: the whole concept of the world's salvation is too great for our finite minds to grasp in our finite lifetime. There is definitely room for a margin of error. If God is great enough to form humankind and establish a plan for us to live, He also can take all of His Words and form them into a basic plot, alphabetized for spirituality, a universal language, and a DNA model for our lives. "Trust in the Lord with all your heart and lean not on your own understanding" (Proverbs 3:5).

Because we do not see the whole picture or understand ourselves, seeking greater knowledge than God's written Word is sinful. There is no greater history book than the Bible. It is not the fact that all of history is found in one book, but the basic model for humankind is described and explained in full detail through God's words. "All Scripture is God-breathed and is useful for teaching, rebuking, correcting and training in righteousness, so that the man of God may be thoroughly equipped for every good work" (2 Timothy 3:16–17).

The Scriptures are God's Word for our souls; therefore, reading is like getting spiritually fed in the same way that a plant would die without food and proper nutrients. This is what happens to humans once they are separated from God. A huge void remains in their hollow souls, and only God's Spirit can sustain them. Reading Scriptures religiously (daily meditations, reflections) is absolutely essential to the spiritual Christian's lifestyle.

Section 3: Fellowship

Her eyes lit up with joy when she saw me. "Tony! Oh my gosh! How long have you been in town?"

"I came in early morning New Year's Eve. I'm visiting my girlfriend's family for the New Year's."

"Oh, that's awesome! What've you been up to?"

"Well, you know the dating lifestyle is challenging. I've been growing. How about you?"

She showed me the ring on her finger and smiled. I had no idea she would be attending the church service that Sunday. It was January 2, 2005 (which happened to be my birthday), and I remembered meeting Pam more than five years earlier with her friends (sisters in Christ) at my college.

"I'm engaged!" she said.

"Wow, that's a beautiful thing!"

"Yeah, we've been together for over three years. I had no idea it was going to happen to me." Her eyes danced with excitement. "He joined the military and was gone for over five months. I wasn't sure if his love would be sustained in the distance." It was over three years after 9/11/01, and our country was in the heart of the War on Terror. "He is so awesome, God is," Pam said. "Who would have known when I saw you that day at U.C.F. [University of Central Florida] while we were praying for our meal, you would be here today, because I witnessed to you and brought you to church. Who would have known that we would be here today while I am engaged and you have a girlfriend, fellowshipping together in God's Kingdom. God is so awesome!"

"Yes, our God is an awesome God!"

I reflect on her words then and now. I remember my friends and family in Christ and God's Kingdom, the bride, His church. We fellowship together and celebrate the beautiful memories and times we spend together. "When you go into battle in your own land against an enemy who is oppressing you, sound a blast on the trumpets. Then you will be remembered by the Lord your God and rescued from your enemies. Also at your times of rejoicing—your appointed feasts and New Moon festivals—you are to sound the trumpets over your burnt offerings and fellowship offerings, and they will be a memorial for you before your God. I am the Lord your God" (Numbers 10:9–10).

Fellowship is the dance of God's Kingdom. As our spirits grow and mature in the faith, our love and brotherhood in the church show and reflect the fact that we are God's people. "Now that you have purified yourselves by obeying the truth so that you have sincere love for your brothers, love one another deeply, from the heart" (1 Peter 1:22). "A new command I give you: Love one another. As I have loved you, so you must love one another. By this all men will know that you are my disciples, if you love one another" (John 13:34–35).

Becoming friends and building friendships, starting new relationships, witnessing, and evangelizing together help form the army of God. We need to fellowship with one another. Men need to join with brothers in prayer, confession of sin, and accountability. Women also need to be growing together with other women. All believers joined together as one in marriage with equal yokes is all part of God's divine plan and evidence of His love for us in His Church.

Section 4: Fasting

"Consider it pure joy, my brothers, whenever you face trials of many kinds, because you know that the testing of your faith develops perseverance. Perseverance must finish its work so that you may be mature and complete, not lacking anything" (James 1:2–4).

If you feel as if I approached the method of having "quiet times" based on "good intentions" and lacked the value of spiritual discipline, then you are mistaken. It happens to be in this particular section that I wish to emphasize the true meaning of self-control and discipline. Nothing is more sacred than preserving your body for God. Many times in our lives, we are confused and unsure of God's faithfulness. It is usually in these times when we lose our good nature and allow ourselves to fall against the mark that He has set for us. Fasting is an awesome way of seeing God's will. "The fear of the Lord is the beginning of knowledge, but fools despise wisdom and discipline" (Proverbs 1:7). "For these commands are a lamp, this teaching is a light, and the corrections of discipline are the way to life" (Proverbs 6:23).

You may see the importance of exercise and good health, but taking yourself to a higher plane spiritually can allow you to feel the presence of God's love through the Holy Spirit. If you lack spiritual vision, then fast. If you want to experience a spiritual connection, then fasting is the best way to gain transmission both physically and spiritually. It is like getting baptized physically while having your soul cleaned spiritually with living water. How does the spiritual realm transform to the physical world? Through faith. "Blessed is he whose transgressions are forgiven, whose sins are covered. Blessed is the man whose sin the Lord does not count against him and in whose spirit is no deceit" (Psalm 32:1–2).

Understanding faith is not trying to live a sinless life; however, because of your relationship with God's Son, Jesus Christ, your sins are forgiven and you are spiritually clean. "Above all, love each other deeply, because love covers over a multitude of sins" (1 Peter 4:8). Fasting helps you stay clean spiritually and to mentally focus on the things that make your spirit grow.

Section 5: Writing

Writing is a passion; like wine tasting, art, the opera, and classical music, it takes an acquired appreciation. I love to write. Perhaps it was the reason that I love to write that I consider it an important habit for a Christian. I write poetry, psalms, and love letters to my mate, and I also keep a personal journal. Although my appetite for writing may be a "haunting conscience" behind my advice to do it as a Christian, it is an awesome practice for you to do, especially if you are young in your Christian faith. Writing down scriptures for memory is a great habit. Now if you desire to write as I do, you may want to write your own prayer requests and/or keep a personal journal. Having some sort of record to reflect on in your spiritual walk is an essence of pure success. Another good practice is to find a pen pal or prayer partner that you can share your growth and struggles, prayers, and blessings with in person or on paper. "Two are better than one, because they have a good return for their work: If one falls down, his friend can help him up. But pity the man who falls and has no one to help him up! Also, if two lie down together, they will keep warm. But how can one keep warm alone? Though one may be overpowered, two can defend themselves. A cord of three strands is not quickly broken" (Ecclesiastes 4:9–12).

If these ideas are not "grabbing" you or you just do not find writing appealing, I strongly suggest you make a personal attempt to at least write down your sinful characteristics or some sins that you struggle with on a daily basis. This is going to give you a target point to focus on when you pray and read scriptures. Writing specific prayers for your personal wicked nature is highly effective. Also, you may even want to write down your blessings to remember humility and place the list on the bathroom or bedroom mirror, the refrigerator door, or any good reminiscing spot. This way you will be able to see and periodically glance at your growth in salvation. You may also write down the prayer requests of your brothers and sisters in Christ, family members, and friends to make them important to you. Nevertheless, regardless of your personal opinion on writing, using it as a practical tool for spiritual development is sagacious.

Section 6: Singing

Have you ever heard a bird sing off key? Or have you heard the sound of crickets chirping out of rhythm? God conducts a symphony in His creation. In the music of the elements, God reflects His harmony and balance of His Holy Spirit. The sound of a bubbling brook or running river, the echoes in the mountains and deep valleys, the falling of hail and rain, and the sound of the mighty wind all are God's perfection, from the evening symphony of crickets to the morning praise of birds. The order and completion of His daily songs are awesome. The infinite wisdom of God understands the finite logic of music theory.

Understanding the balance and harmony can help us attain peace and holiness in our own spirits. We come to harmony with God and hear His music in nature. Harmony means agreement like matching colors or proper notes on a keyboard. This agreement between the heart and the spirit is essential to the communication of God and man. God does talk to us; however, an unraveled spirit cannot hear Him or comprehend His pure and gentle sound. "But the wicked are like the tossing sea, which cannot rest, whose waves cast up mire and mud" (Isaiah 57:20).

"Honest scales and balances are from the Lord; all the weights in the bag are of his making" (Proverbs 16:11). God weighs the spirit of the heart and soul. Man uses his finite mind and limited knowledge to balance his spirit between his heart and soul; however, God's nature is pure, gentle, and holy. He has perfect balance in His being and spirit. Even the colors are arranged to reflect the harmony and balance of light and sound. This balance of sight and sound allows us to react to this world. Having the ability to see spiritual colors of life with your heart reveals a mature soul. Watching a sunset, seeing the colors of birds, noticing butterflies and flowers, and seeing a smile on someone's face all play a role in God's gift of pictures of life.

Singing is coming to grips with the peace that transcends through one's spirit. You can embrace it within an order of mental sound and balance. If you cannot fathom seeing yourself sing, even church hymns or gospel, you can simply listen to music. It is like understanding the reason that one can't be melancholy while laughing. Music releases the fire from within your soul and engulfs the aura with joy. When you are singing, you can't allow room in your heart for hatred. Even an angry song pleases the audience when you find solidarity with it, although the style of music you listen to can pervert your spirit if it is in discord. As light illumines the spirit from darkness, music brings comfort to the soul, even in the smallest shadow of one's character.

Section 7: Tithing

The money—it's all about the money; money talks; the root of all evil is the love of money. Why should I even mention money when referring to a relationship with God? Why would I end a book on daily devotions with a section on money?

Actually, the truth is that I don't believe that tithing pertains only to economic value. I believe the key to tithing is sacrifice or putting God first. You must make some kind of sacrifice to please God and put Him first. This sacrifice can be measured with monetary values; however, you can tithe with service in the community or church. You can volunteer your personal gifts from God to the community (as I offer poetry and have friends who play music for concerts and others who cook and cater food for fellowship). You may feel as if you may be cheating God if you do not financially pay some tithe—ten percent, to be exact. And, to tell the truth, those who tithe financially are rewarded greatly. Nevertheless, if you read through my entire book and believe this is the proper mentality to have when it comes to serving God (that you have to pay ten percent of your income), then I seriously failed in my attempt to lead you spiritually. It is what is in your heart that counts; it is all about the heart.

"Jesus sat down opposite the place where the offerings were put and watched the crowd putting their money into the temple treasury. Many rich people threw in large amounts. But a poor widow came and put in two very small copper coins, worth only a fraction of a penny. Calling his disciples to him, Jesus said, 'I tell you the truth, this poor widow has put more into the treasury than all the others. They all gave out of their wealth; but she, out of her poverty, put in everything—all she had to live on'" (Mark 12:41–44).

"Then he said to them all: "If anyone would come after me, he must deny himself and take up his cross daily and follow me. For whoever wants to save his life will lose it, but whoever loses his life for me will save it. What good is it for a man to gain the whole world, and yet lose or forfeit his very self?" (Luke 9:23–25).

"Remember this: Whoever sows sparingly will also reap sparingly, and whoever sows generously will also reap generously. Each man should give what he has decided in his heart to give, not reluctantly or under compulsion, for God loves a cheerful giver" (2 Corinthians 9:6–7).

I am pleased to leave this controversial topic to close the matters of how I feel in the heart about God and religion. Yes, you may feel that I am wrong, and that is exactly how I want the picture to look. On one hand, we have the legalistic concept of what is right and wrong; and on the other hand, we have the "grayness" of life's black and white issues. What is right? Spirituality needs to be accepted personally for it to make sense. I honestly hope that you leave this book still unsure about what I feel is right. It is all about the heart, my dear readers; it is all about the heart.

www.ingramcontent.com/pod-product-compliance
Ingram Content Group UK Ltd.
Pitfield, Milton Keynes, MK11 3LW, UK
UKHW041949230426
12048UKWH00008B/235